Henry Edward Turner

Jeremy Clarke's Family

An Address Before the Rhode Island Historical Society

Henry Edward Turner

Jeremy Clarke's Family
An Address Before the Rhode Island Historical Society

ISBN/EAN: 9783337379940

Printed in Europe, USA, Canada, Australia, Japan

Cover: Foto ©ninafisch / pixelio.de

More available books at **www.hansebooks.com**

JEREMY CLARKE'S FAMILY.

AN ADDRESS

BEFORE THE

RHODE ISLAND HISTORICAL SOCIETY

MARCH, 1879.

By H. E. TURNER.

[REPRINTED FROM THE NEWPORT HISTORICAL MAGAZINE.]

NEWPORT HISTORICAL PUBLISHING COMPANY.

J. E. SANBORN, PRINTER, 1881.

JEREMY CLARKE'S FAMILY.

ADDRESS DELIVERED BEFORE R. I. HISTORICAL SOCIETY, MARCH, 1879, BY H. E. TURNER.

I have had the honor heretofore of addressing you on the relations of the Greenes of Warwick, and of Governor William Coddington, of Newport, to the public affairs of the Colony of Rhode Island and Providence Plantations, and more particularly from the settlement to the year 1700.

In so doing I have taken particular pains that every proposition made by me should be sustained by documentary evidence, quoted at full length, and with entire fullness and impartiality. And so far as I may be allowed to judge myself, I have divested myself of prejudice and arrived at the views which I have expressed, without bias.

The views of the colonists were various, as are those of men at all periods, one party being more or less reactionary, while the other was more or less disposed to extreme liberal, and in some cases, probably revolutionary, tendencies. I have treated Coddington as the representative of the former, the Greenes of the latter.

I propose now to pursue the subject by the introduction of a family, two generations of whom were emphatically and very prominently identified with every movement towards the strengthening of the popular element in their institutions, and the reduction of the predominant influence of the Court and the Parliament in colonial affairs, and toward resisting the aggressive spirit constantly exhibited by their more populous and powerful neighbors. I refer to Jeremiah Clarke, or Jeremy, as he is usually called in the records, and his descendants, of whom, as I

shall have occasion to show, very many, not inheriting his name, have been prominent and influential in our history.

I should here, perhaps, eliminate John Clarke, whose personal importance and influence, at the same period, are universally acknowledged, and are worthy of extended study, from this discussion, inasmuch as no connection is known or supposed to have existed between the two families, each of which became very numerous; John's, through his brothers, he leaving no children.

I have been able to find no account of the "locum tenens" of Jeremiah Clarke before leaving England, nor do the records of Massachusetts or Plymouth show that he made any settlement in either of those colonies, nor does his name appear among the signers of the compact at Pocasset [Portsmouth], March 7, 1638, but his name appears as being present at a general meeting at Portsmouth, Jan. 2, 1638-9, and next his name appears affixed to the following agreement which resulted in the settlement at Newport, viz., April 28, 1639:

"It is agreed
" By us, whose hands are underwritten, to propagate
" a plantation in the midst of the Island or elsewhere;
" and do engage ourselves to bear equal charges, answer-
" able to our strength and estates in common; and that
" our determinations shall be by major voice of judge and
" elders; the judge to have a double voice."

" Present :
"Wm. Coddington, Judge,   "John Clarke,
"Nicholas Easton,   ⎫   "Jeremiah Clarke,
"John Coggeshall,   ⎬ Elders. "Thomas Hazard,
"William Brenton,   ⎭   "Henry Bull,
               "William Dyre, Clerk."

Mr. Clarke held the following offices:
Military—Lieutenant, 1642; Captain, 1644.

Civil—Constable, 1639; Treasurer of Portsmouth, 1644 to 1647; Treasurer of Providence Plantations, 1647 to 1649.

In May, 1648, Wm. Coddington having been elected Governor of Providence Plantations under the patent to which Rhode Island had subscribed the previous year, and having been suspended from the functions of the office until he should clear himself from certain charges, Mr. Clarke was elected to supply his place, and administered the government during that year, under the title of President Regent.

The particular charges against Governor Coddington are not of record, and therefore we are left to conjecture as to their precise character, but we have reason to suppose that they grew out of his declared hostility to the Gortonian settlement, and his disapproval of the union with Providence and Warwick, under the charter of 1643, which view is fortified by the pregnant circumstances of his visit to England in the winter following, and his return in 1651 with a commission constituting him Governor for life of the islands.

The active agency of Jeremiah Clarke in this affair is plainly shown by the significant fact, that he was selected to fill the place thus made vacant, but it is confirmed by the following quotation from Roger Williams' letter to John Winthrop, Junior (Winthrop papers, Mass. Hist. Soc. Coll., Vol. 9, p. 278, viz.):

"Our poor colony is in civil dissension, their last meet-
"ings, at which I have not been, have fallen into factions,
"Mr. Coddington and Captain Partridge the heads of one;
"Captain Clarke and Mr. Easton the heads of the other
"faction. I receive letters from both, inviting me, &c.,
"but I resolve, if the Lord please, not to be engaged, un-

"less with great hopes of peacemaking; the peace makers
"are the sons of God."

The materials for a biography of Governor Clarke are
very meagre; they are chiefly to be derived from the public records, and in this case we have especial reason to deplore and condemn the unwise and unjustifiable action of
the General Assembly, at the March session, 1656, the
record of which is as follows (R. I. Col. Rec., Vol. 1, p.
332):

"Whereas, there were certain transactions which were
"done in ye time of Mr. Coddington his government, and
"stood in our book of record, which might seem prejudi-
"cial to himself or others. It being much considered in
"ye case, this Court not thinking it fit to meddle with it,
"ordered that it should be cut out of our book, which was
"done, and then delivered to Mr. Coddington."

As a result of this act, there is a hiatus in our colonial records as regards Newport and Portsmouth, from May,
1649, to May, 1653. This includes the period during
which Gov. Clarke, as the acknowledged leader of what
Roger Williams calls the faction against Gov. Coddington's schemes, must have been especially active and prominent, and doubtless the record so ordered expurgated,
would have been very useful to our present purpose, and
would have contributed very materially in illuminating
a period exceptionally obscure.

After 1649, when he served his last term as Treasurer,
Gov. Clarke held no colonial office. He died in 1661, at
which time his wife was 50 years of age, and we may suppose that his age did not differ very much from hers.

His wife was Frances, daughter of Louis Latham, and
widow of Thomas Dougan, by whom she had two daughters: Barbara, who married James Barker, and Margaret.
After the death of Gov. Clarke she married a third hus-

band, Rev. Wm. Vaughan, the first pastor of the Second Baptist church in Newport. She died September, 1677, aged 66 years.

A fond delusion has fostered a romantic tradition that Louis Latham was a natural son of Charles I., but as Charles was born about 1600, and Frances Latham in 1611, we can hardly entertain much faith in a legend which makes him her grandfather.

The children of Jeremiah and Frances Clarke were:

I. Frances,[2] born 1638, married Randall Holden.
II. Walter,[2] born 1640, died May 22, 1714; married
   1st, Content; she d. March 27, 1665-6, aged 30 yrs.
   2d, Hannah Scott; she d. July 24, 1681, aged 39 yrs.
   3d, Freeborn Hart, daughter of R. Williams; she d. Dec. 10, 1709.
   4th, Sarah Prior, of Matthew, widow of John Gould, married Aug. 31, 1711.
III. Mary,[2] born 1641, died April 7, 1711, aged 69 years, m.
   1st, Gov. John Cranston; he d. March 12, 1680, aged 54 years.
   2d, John Stanton.
IV. Jeremiah,[2] born 1643; married Ann Audley.
V. Latham,[2] born 1645, died June 1, 1719, married
   1st, Hannah Wilbour, of Samuel.
   2d, Anne Newberry, widow of Walter, Sept. 20, 1698; she died Feb. 19, 1732, aged 80 yrs. 6 m
VI. Weston,[2] born July 2, 1648, married
   1st, Mary Easton, of Peter, Dec. 25, 1668; she d. Nov. 16, 1690, aged 42 years.
   2d, Rebecca Easton, widow of Peter, Jr., daughter of Edward Thurston, Nov. 21, 1691; she died Sept. 16, 1737, aged 75 years, 4 months.
VII. James,[2] born 1649, died Dec. 1, 1736, aged 87 yrs., m. Hope Power, of Nicholas, of Providence; she died Feb. 27, 1717-8, aged 67 years.

6   *Jeremy Clarke's Family.*

VIII. Sarah,[2] born 1651, died —— —— ——, married Gov. Caleb Carr, of Newport, 2d wife.

Two of Gov. Clarke's sons-in-law were governors of the colony, as also his son Walter and his grandson, Samuel Cranston. Among his descendants who have been honored by election as governors of Rhode Island, is the second Wm. Greene of Warwick, making six of his family who have filled that high position, as follows, viz:

Jeremiah Clarke,	1 yr.
Walter Clarke, son of Jeremiah,	4 yrs.
John Cranston, son-in-law of Jeremiah,	2 yrs.
Caleb Carr, son-in-law of Jeremiah,	1 yr.
Samuel Cranston, grandson of Jeremiah,	29 yrs.
Wm. Greene, 1st, m. Catherine Greene. gr. gr. gr. daughter,	11 yrs.
Wm. Greene, 2d, 5th generation in descent,	8 yrs.
	56 yrs.

Those of his family who have been Deputy or Lieut. Governors of Rhode Island, are six, viz:

John Cranston, son-in-law,	3 yrs.
Walter Clarke, son,	21 yrs.
John Gardner, married Frances Sanford, granddaughter,	9 yrs.
Wm. Greene, 1st, married Catherine Greene, 4th generation,	1 yr.
Wm. Greene, 7th generation,	2 yrs.
Samuel G. Arnold,	3 yrs.
	39 yrs.

The term of service of the 2d Gov. Greene closed in May, 1786, therefore, from the union of the towns in 1647 to 1786, one hundred and thirty-nine years, the seat had been occupied 56 years by members of this family, to which might properly be added the three years of the

Andros usurpation, when Walter Clarke being the incumbent, may be regarded as legally Governor, making 59 years; this leaves 80 years for others. During that period, not improbably, some of the more recent incumbents with whose families I am not familiar, are also of the same stock, for the extent to which the blood of Jeremiah Clarke permeated the community of native Rhode Islanders is a perfect marvel.

During the first 100 years, or from 1647 to 1747, this family held the governorship 44 years, including the suspension of the Charter, leaving 56 years for others to occupy it. During the same time they held the Deputy Governorship 27 years.

These facts show conclusively the paramount influence of the Clarkes and their connections in colonial affairs, and prove that they enjoyed in a pre-eminent degree, the confidence and respect of the people. I shall endeavor to present the facts my limited opportunities afford me, in such a manner as to prove that such confidence and respect were, in the main, well deserved.

At the May session of the Assembly, 1648, Captain Clarke and Mr. Barton were appointed to carry a letter to ye Bay (Massachusetts), and receive their answer concerning Warwick business.

Jeremy Clarke was a witness to the deed of Misquannacook, now Westerly, June 29, 1660.

Walter Clarke, the eldest son of Jeremiah, was born in 1640, and died May 22, 1714. He was Governor of the Colony in 1676-7, and from May, 1680, to June, 1686, "de facto," and from June, 1686, to February, 1690, "de jure;" also from May, 1695, to May, 1698. He was Deputy Governor from 1679 to 1686, and from 1700 to 1714, holding both offices 27 years, the latter at the time of his decease. He was a Deputy from Newport in 1672-3-4, and Assistant in 1675.

In October, 1672, on Auditing Committee.
In May, 1673, on committee to supervise the election.
In May, 167 , on committee to supervise the election.

Walter Clarke to Edward Randolph :—
"Esteemed and courteous: Understanding by the
"blessing of God, of thy landing at Boston, the 13th
"instant, hold myself obliged to congratulate thy safe
"arrival once more into these American parts, and to as-
"sure thee that as I stand constituted in my present ca-
"pacity, shall be glad to serve thee in any office of love
"in my power, which, I presume, is the minds of all my
"well beloved friends, and hope our practice will de-
"monstrate the same, if time and opportunity offer.
"Having a true regard to all such whom his Majesty, in
"his princely wisdom, thinks meet to employ in his weighty
"concerns, is all at present, and with dear respects to all
"so immediately concerned,

"Remain thy assured friend,
"WALTER CLARKE.
"Newport on Rhode Island, this 15th day, 3d mo., 1686."
[R. I. Col. Rec., Vol. 3, p. 198, from Mass. Hist. Coll., Vol. 8, p. 179.]

In order to form any estimate of the character of Walter Clarke, we must bear in mind that he was a Quaker of the primitive type; that he was a personal disciple of George Fox; and that he derived his peculiar religious ideas from his own lips; and we must remember that the Quakers of those days were very rigid in the tenacity with which they adhered to their doctrines, and the discipline by which they were held to them, by their association was very severe; and also that they had not begun to relay their discipline in any degree, so that any observations made in this generation, where we have seen the Quakers gradually relaxing in their ideas until they have almost

become homogeneous with world's people, can give very little aid in estimating the difficulties likely to arise from the conflict between their notions and those of other men.

The doctrine of non-resistance, which forbade any resort to violence, could not fail, in a peculiarly turbulent and stormy period, to occasion frequent complications difficult to disentangle, unless we keep constantly in view these circumstances.

From 1670 to 1698, except for one year, when Benedict Arnold was Governor, that office was held by members of that society, so that whenever any warlike measures were necessary to be taken, even by requisitions from the Crown, some subordinate officer took the matter in hand and issued commissions, as in the case of Deputy Governor John Greene.

The predominance of Quaker councils may explain the apparent readiness with which the Rhode Island authorities recognized the authority of Sir Edmond Andros, which their subsequent conduct showed must have been entirely repugnant to their views.

The first act of Walter Clarke, as Governor, which appears in the Colonial Records, is a commission with his signature to Captain Arthur Fenner, as "Chief Commander of the King's Garrison at Providence," which garrison was established in view of the Indian troubles, at May session, 1676, and consisted of seven men, with a commander, at six shillings a week money for the men, and twelve for the commander, two men to be added at the cost of the owner of the house occupied as the garrison house, making the whole number ten men. This garrison was ordered to be supplied with one great gun belonging to the owners of the ship Newport, with fifty pounds of

powder and one hundred weight of lead *et seq'r.*
[R. I. Col. Rec., Vol 2, p. 546.]

Probably at this time Walter Clarke had not yet become a convert to the tenets of George Fox.

The next act to which his name appears affixed, is
" An address from the Governor and Company of Rhode
" Island, to James the Second, on the receipt of the Quo
" Warranto as follows:

" To his most excellent Majesty, Our Sovereign Lord,
" James the Second. The humble address of the Gover-
" nor and Company of your Majesty's Colony of Rhode
" Island and Providence Plantations, in New England, in
" America:

" Most Dread Sovereign: We, your Majesty's most
" dutiful and loyal subjects do, with all humble and due
" submission, prostrate ourselves and privileges at your
" Majesty's feet, humbly acknowledge your Majesty's gra-
" cious favour. In your Royal letters of the 26th of June,
" 1685, in the first year of your reign, directed to our hon-
" ored Governor, wherein you are graciously pleased to
" signify 'we shall, at all times, extend our Royal care
" and protection to them, in the preservation of their
" rights and in the defence and security of their persons
" and estates, which we think fit that you signify unto the
" inhabitants of that your colony', we, your Majesty's
" most dutiful subjects, humbly acknowledge the receipt
" of your Quo Warrantos, by the hand of Edward Ran-
" dolph, Esq., against the Charter of your Majesty's said
" Colony, which we received the 22d June, 1686, requir-
" ing our appearance before his Majesty, wherever he shall
" then be, in England, to answer from the day of Easter
" in fifteen days, which time had its period before the re-
" ception of the same, which was the 22d day of June,
" 1686. Notwithstanding, in obedience to your gracious

"Majesty's commands, your Governor and Company con-
"vened, and upon serious consideration thereof, saw cause
"forthwith to publish and declare, by open proclamation,
"that they would not stand suit with your Majesty, but
"to address themselves to your most excellent Majesty for
"favour and relief, praying and imploring your Princely
"bounty in our said Charter, contained both in religious
"and civil concernments; and the rather, that we are a
"people that have been and are real to the Royal interest,
"and despised by our neighboring Colonies. May it please
"your Majesty to know that before we received a Quo
"Warranto, or so much as a copy of your Majesty's Com-
"mission to the honored President, Joseph Dudley, Esq.,
"that the greater part of our Colony was assumed from
"us, called the King's Province, which we did not oppose.

"And farther, we beg that in your Princely clemency,
"you will please to continue our privileges in *statu quo
"privis*, with respect to indulgence in matters of religious
"concernments, and forming of catches (oaths) and attes-
"tations.

"And farther, we humbly petition your Royal favour,
"that forasmuch as the port of Newport, on Rhode Island,
"lays in the heart of all your Majesty's Colonies, it may
"be a free port for navigation and entries, paying duties.

"And farther, we beg your Majesty's most gracious fa-
"vour herein, that no persons may be imposed over us that
"suit not the nature and constitution of your Majesty's
"subjects here, which our late Majesty of blessed memory
"was graciously pleased to indulge us in.

"And finally, we pray your gracious Majesty, that in all
"things wherein we have been weak or short, through ig-
"norance, may be remitted and pardoned; and cannot but
"think that through the disaffection of some, many things
"have been misrepresented. All which is humbly sub-

"mitted, and we beseech your most Excellent Majesty to
"accept hereof, prostrating our all at your gracious feet,
"with our entire resolutions to serve our Sovereign with
"faithful hearts, praying for your Majesty's long life and
"prosperous reign over us. And remain your Majesty's
"legal subjects and supplicants."
(Signed) "WALTER CLARKE, Governor.
"Newport, on Rhode Island, the 3d of July, 1686."
[R. I. Col. Rec., Vol. 3, pp. 193-4.]

This address may seem to us to have been couched in terms unnecessarily humble and submissive, and we should feel better pleased, perhaps, to have seen exhibited a more belligerent spirit on their part, but we must consider that the reign of James Second commenced with many evidences of strength. As Admiral of the British navy, he had been very popular, and his good natured brother, Charles Second, had kept up peculiarly friendly relations with this colony, and in fact his administration had been generally indulgent and kindly in its relations with all the colonies; that the claims of the colony to royal favor might have been seriously damaged by a contest with the crown, while the probability of an equitable and favorable adjudication before a court constituted by the adverse party for the specific object whose accomplishment they would be engaged in contesting, at very great pains and expense, was too limited for the indulgence of hope.

If the united colonies, Massachusetts, Plymouth, New Haven and Connecticut, with their combined power and influence, declined such a contest, we may readily conclude that little Rhode Island could ill afford to enter into a demonstration which, by no possibility, could result in anything but defeat and disaster. We are not, therefore, to suppose that the hearts of the colonists were fully in accord with their expressions, particularly as their subsequent acts show a sturdy resistance to the aggressions of

the Crown, upon the rights and privileges they believed to be guaranteed by the Royal Charter, which charter was, during the period of its abeyance, in the custody of Walter Clarke himself.

We are rather to admire the address with which they gained the good will of James and his courtly representatives, and the good sense and good faith they exhibited in their orderly behavior under the Andros administration, which was doubtless extremely distasteful to them. So acceptable was their carriage, that of seven members of the legislative council nominated by Sir Edmond, four at least were of the liberal party, to wit: Clarke, Greene, Coggeshall, and Newberry.

In response to Mr. Randolph's charges and specifications, an order in council was issued, of date July 15, 1685, as follows, viz.:

"COUNCIL CHAMBER, 15th July, 1685.

"His Majesty being graciously pleased to approve the "same, is pleased to order and direct that the said Articles "be, and they are hereby referred to Sir Robert Sawyer, "Knight, his Majesty's Attorney General, who is forth- "with to bring writs of Quo Warranto ag' 'st the Gov- "ernor and Company of the Colony of Connecticut, and "the Governor and Company of Rhode Island and Prov- "idence Plantations, in New England.

"And it is further ordered, that Mr. Attorney General "do forthwith consider of the several grants and proprie- "tors (proprietaries possibly) of East and West New Jer- "sey, and of Delaware, and enter the like writs of Quo "Warranto against the respective proprietors thereof, if "he shall have just cause.

(Signed) "WILLIAM BRIDGMAN."

To this was appended the following, viz.:

"Mem: My Lord President is desired by the Right

"Honorable the Lords of the Committee for Trade and Plantations, to move his Majesty, that the directions to Mr. Attorney General, that the prosecution of several writs of Quo Warranto against the propriety of the Province of Maryland, and against the proprietors of East and West New Jersey, and of Delaware, in America, may be renewed, and that the same may be prosecuted to effect."

"Council Chamber, 21st April, 1686."

[R. I. Col. Rec., Vol. 3, p. 177.]

This prosecution was ordered then, two months and one day before the respondents were required to answer to it, at a period when two months was the ordinary time for one passage across the Atlantic. This manner of dealing shows, emphatically, the utter disregard which the government meant to exhibit of any pretence of respect for the rights or wishes of the colonists.

[R. I. Col. Rec. Vol. 3, p. 177, from N. Y. Documents, Vol. 3, p. 362.]

In the Royal Instructions to Sir Edmond Andros dated Sept. 13, 1686, we read as follows:

"Whereas, we have been presented with the humble address of our Governor and Colony of Rhode Island and Providence Plantations, within our Territory and dominion of New England, bearing date the 3d day of June last, wherein they take notice of our writ of Quo Warranto against their Charter, and thereupon declaring their resolution not to stand suit with us, have submitted themselves and their Charter to our Royal determination. Our will and pleasure is, and we do hereby authorize and empower you, upon your arrival in those parts, to demand, in our name, the surrender of their

" said Charter into your hands, in pursuance of their said
" declaration and address ", &c.
[R. I. Col. Rec., Vol. 3, p. 218, from Mass. Hist. Coll.,
Vol. 7, p. 162.]

In accordance with these instructions, on the 22d of December, 1686, Sir Edmond writes the Governor, Walter Clarke, as follows:

"BOSTON, Dec. 22, 1686.

" SIR: This is to acquaint you that I arrived yester-
" day, at which time his Majesty's Commission, bearing
" date at Windsor, the third day of June last, in the sec-
" ond year of his reign, appointed me Captain General and
" Governor in Chief of his territory and dominion of New
" England, and his Majesty having, upon the address and
" submission of the Charter, accepted thereof, hath com-
" manded and authorized me, upon my arrival in these
" parts, to demand, in his Majesty's name, the actual sur-
" render of the said Charter, and to take the Colony of
" Rhode Island and Providence Plantations into my care,
" as part of the Government", &c.

Under these circumstances we must infer that the Charter was delivered to the Royal Governor, and yet, on the 27th February, 1690, the General Assembly appointed a Committee to demand of Walter Clarke, the late Governor, the Charter, &c., which he declined to give up, unless they forced the chest in which they were kept, which they accordingly did.

The only explanation of which these circumstances are susceptible,is,that Sir E. Andros received a duplicate copy, and yet how could the existence of another copy have escaped the cognizance of the numerous and prominent members of the Charter Government who openly and actively abetted the encroachments of the Crown?

No elucidation of these somewhat mystical transactions

is necessary to satisfy us, that whether a pious fraud was perpetrated on the Hon. Viceroy, or a pertinacious and stubborn courage was exercised by the honored representative of Jeremiah Clarke, we are in either case deeply indebted to him for the preservation of the sacred instrument which enabled our ancestors to restore their own rights and liberties, and to reorganize the institutions under which they and we lived and prospered for a century and a half thereafter.

Another address was made by certain inhabitants of Rhode Island and Providence Plantations, bearing date July 16th, 1686, thirteen days later than the submission by the Governor and Company, which, after making a similar submission, proceeds :

" And whereas, the General Assembly of your Majesty's
" aforesaid Colony, sitting the 29th of June, 1686, have
" made their public declaration that they will not stand
" suit with your Majesty, but will proceed, by their hum-
" ble address, for continuation of their privileges and lib-
" erties according to the Charter, and that many of the
" freemen did give in their judgment to the Assembly, and
" left the further proceedings to their judicious determina-
" tion, as by their declaration herewith sent, may appear.

"We, your present supplicants and humble petitioners,
" declare that we know nothing of it, neither have we left
" the further proceedings with the Assembly, but pre-
" sent ourselves before your Majesty, by this, our early
" and humble address, desiring we may be discharged of all
" levies and contributions which they would expose us to,
" to defray the charges of an agent going for England,
" to which we cannot consent, and shall ever pray for
" your Majesty's long and happy reign.

" Your Majesty's most loyal and obedient subjects,
" Jno. Williams,
" Thomas Coddington,

" Josiah Arnold,
" Francis Brinley,
" Richard Smith,
" Edward Pelham,
" Nathaniel Coddington,
" Christopher Almy,
" Peleg Sanford,
" John Fones,
" John Odlin,
" Andrew Willett,
" John Greene of [Quidnesett],
his
"John J. R. Rathbone,
marke."

[R. I. Col. Rec., Vol. 3, pp. 194-5, from J. Carter Brown's Manuscripts. Vol. 4, Nos. 207-8.]

The difference in the tone and spirit of this uncalled for address, from the dignified and self-respecting missive of the Colonial authorities, is too patent to escape the most superficial observation. It is, in fact, a repudiation of the Charter and the authority of those who acted under it, and an unreserved abnegation of all the muniments and benefits secured by it, and an abject renunciation of all the security to personal rights in which all true Englishmen had for centuries been striving to intrench themselves against the arbitrary exercise of the Royal authority.

As the name of John Greene appears among the subscribers to this document, I take leave to show that John Greene, of Warwick, afterwards Deputy Governor, was not, and could not be the person in question; first, because he was at the time one of the assistants; second, because he was one of the committee appointed to draw up and forward the legislative address, which committee was composed as follows, viz.:

"Our honored Governor and Deputy Governor for New-
"port; Mr. Joseph Jenckes for Providence; Mr. Peleg
"Tripp and the Recorder for Portsmouth; Major John
"Greene for Warwick." [R. I. Col. Rec., Vol. 3, p. 192.]

Third, because he was, probably, the agent employed to carry and present the address, and he is known to have been in London in the following January.

Fourth, because the other names attached to the paper are those of the very men with whom he had been in lifelong conflict. They represent the party which supported Coddington in the warfare against the prevalence of the Patent of 1643, and his authority under his perpetual commission, that resisted the extension of Rhode Island authority over the King's province, with all the energy and persistence they could exert; and they afterwards abetted Earl Bellomont in all his efforts to extend the Royal prerogative. On the other hand, John Greene, of Quidnesett, was always "art and part" with them, especially in the effort to procure the assignment of King's province to Connecticut. We may, therefore, consider the name of John Greene, of Warwick, as eliminated from this association, and that of his namesake substituted.

Our space is too limited to admit of any discussion of Sir Edmond's administration, suffice it; that it was regarded with unlimited detestation by all the colonists of liberal sentiments, not only in Rhode Island, but in all the other colonies under his government, that all public rights and claims were overruled for the aggrandizement of an army of place-holders, imported from England, to prey upon the resources of the colonists, and of such inhabitants of the country as were sufficiently abject in their sycophancy to conciliate the Viceroyal favor. We find, accordingly, that immediately on the announcement of the deposition of King James, Sir Edmond and his satellites were

seized at Boston and put under surveillance, and his authority renounced by all the colonies of New England, and the functions of government resumed under the original Charters by the colonists themselves.

Abundant authority for these strong expressions may be found in original papers published in Hon. J. R. Bartlett's R. I. Colonial Records, Vol. 3, and in the Andros tracts published by the Prince Society of Boston. These materials are worthy of laborious analysis and extensive elucidation.

Our present purpose is simply to give the facts, so far as they connect themselves with Walter Clarke, and to speculate on them, only in a very limited degree.

On the fourth of April, 1689, it was whispered in Boston, that a Protestant revolution had taken place in England. On the eighteenth, divers of the prominent citizens of Boston addressed Sir Edmond Andros, advising him that he had better surrender himself and his associates and the fortifications about Boston, in order to secure their own safety and obviate the impending effusion of blood. This was followed by the imprisonment of those gentlemen and the restoration of the Charter Government in Massachusetts.

The latest record which appears of acts in Rhode Island under the Andros administration, is as follows:

"At a General Quarter Sessions, held at Newport, for "Rhode Island, King's Province and Providence Planta- "tions, the 11th day of December, 1688.

"Justices Present,

"Francis Brinley,   "John Coggeshall,
"Peleg Sanford,   "Caleb Carr, Sen'r,
"Richard Smith,   "Arthur Fenner,
          "John Fones," &c.
              [R. I. Col. Rec., Vol. 3, p. 245.]

Five days after the grand demonstration in Boston, the following call was issued to the people of Rhode Island, emanating undoubtedly from Walter Clarke and John Coggeshall, the last Governor and Deputy Governor under the Charter, though only signed with their initials, viz.:

"Whereas, we have seen a printed paper dated from
" Boston, the 18th of April last, which signifieth that Sir
" Edmond Andros, our late Governor, with several others,
" are seized and confined, so that many of the free people
" of this place are bent to lay hold on their former privi-
" leges:
" Neighbors and Friends, we therefore cannot omit to rec-
" ommend unto you our present grievance, to wit: that we
" are sufficiently informed that our late government, under
" which we were subservient, is now silenced and eclipsed;
" we, under a sense of our deplorable and unsettled condi-
" tion, do offer to you, whether it may not be expedient for
" the several towns of this late Colony, the several prin-
" cipal persons therein, to make their personal appearance
" at Newport, before the day of usual election by Charter,
" which will be the first day of May next, there to consult
" and agree, of some suitable way, in this present junc-
" ture, and whether our ancient privileges and former
" methods may not be best to insist upon, which we leave
" to your judicious consideration, and that you may not
" say you were ignorant, but had the most timeliest no-
" tice that could be given at so little warning, is all at
" present from your real friends and neighbours.

"W——— C———,
"J ——— C———.

" Newport, this 23d April, 1689."

[R. I. Col. Rec., Vol. 3, p. 257.]

To this Mr. Bartlett appends the following note:

" The paper from which the foregoing copy is made,

"was received at Providence from Newport. It appears
"to be the original, and is in the handwriting of Walter
"Clarke. The letter itself is very cautiously drawn, and
"there is no notice of its reception upon the Town Rec-
"ords."
This paper was signed by Walter Clarke, and also is in
his handwriting, and it expresses, in a very cautious manner, his wish that the people should reinstate the Charter
Government, but for some reason to which the records
give us no clue, he appears to have declined any very positive action under the restoration, of which the following
papers furnish the only tangible evidence, until May,
1690, when he declined a reëlection. Perhaps his religious or conscientious scruples prevented his reassuming
power after so long an interval, without a reëlection according to the call above transcribed, and there is no evidence of any such election having been held, or of any
public record having been kept from the abdication of Sir
Edmond Andros, April 18, 1689, until February 26, 1689-
90, except as I shall hereafter show, more than ten months
after, when a session of the General Assembly was held
at Newport. At this session were present :
"Major John Coggeshall, Deputy Governor.
ASSISTANTS :
"Mr. John Easton, "Mr. George Lawton,
" Mr. Edward Thurston, " Major John Greene,
" Mr. Joseph Jenckes, " Mr. Benjamin Smith,
" Recorder, " General Serjeant,
" Mr. Weston Clarke, " Mr. Thomas Frye."
These assistants are the same who were elected in May,
1686, and in the same order, except Mr. Benjamin Smith,
who was elected June 29, 1686, in place of Samuel Stafford, declined, and omitting Messrs. Newberry, Fenner, and
Richard Arnold. Mr. Newberry probably had scruples
identical with Walter Clarke, being, like him, a prominent

disciple of George Fox, and having like him, accepted service in Sir Edmond Andros' Council, as appears by the record of the first Council of Andros, at Boston, Dec. 30, 1686, as follows, after the oath had been administered to the other members of the Council, among whom were John Coggeshall, Richard Arnold, and John Albro, from Rhode Island, viz. :

"Walter Clarke and Walter Newberry gave also their "express consent to the oath of allegiance, and the oath "for the administration of justice in the government, ac- "cording as directed in his Majesty's late Commission to "the President and Council, professing themselves obliged "in all good conscience before God so to do, and that, "under the utmost penalties of perjury in all respects, the "members of the Council, being severally asked their "opinion, did allow of their protestation. His Excellen- "cy, in short discourse, encouraged the members to free- "dom in debates. Walter Clarke and Walter Newberry "acknowledge the surrender of the Charter made to his "Majesty at Windsor, but fearing that surrender was not "effectual for avoiding all mistakes, they had presented "another humble address to his Majesty, under the public "seal of their Colony, and had sent over agents to pray his "Majesty's favor towards them, and W. Clarke further "added, the Charter of Rhode Island was in his custody "at Newport." [R. I. Col. Rec., Vol. 3, pp. 220-1, from Mass. Hist Coll., Vol. 7, pp. 162-4-6, and Vol. 8, p. 180.]

JEREMY CLARKE'S FAMILY.

ADDRESS DELIVERED BEFORE THE R. I. HISTORICAL SOCIETY, MARCH, 1879, BY H. E. TURNER.

CHAPTER II.

Without disparagement to Coggeshall, who had taken an oath to the same effect, we may not only excuse, but honor, the integrity of Clarke and Newberry, who, in the face of such an obligation and renunciation as this, refused to act three years later on their election of May, 1686, and the circumstances give no warrant for the expression of a distinguished historian, quoted by Mr. Bartlett, that Walter Clarke wavered. Had an election been held in May, 1689, as he proposed, and had he at that time been elected, he would probably have considered his difficulties removed. For what reasons he declined to act, ten months later, it is not necessary to enquire; it is somewhat to our purpose, however, that he was urged so to act in February, 1689-90, because it shows that his failure to act in the preceding year had not displeased the freemen, but that, on the contrary, he enjoyed their fullest confidence.

The papers above referred to as showing that Walter

Clarke did not act as Governor from May, 1689, to May, 1690, are these:

"From the Governor and Council of Rhode Island to
"their Majesties, William and Mary, of England:

" Most dread Sovereigns:—We, your Majesties' most
" humble subjects and supplicants of your colony of Rhode
" Island and Providence Plantations, in New England,
" having received the joyful tidings of both your Majes-
" ties' safe arrival in England, after your so great and haz-
" ardous undertaking for the good of the nation, to relieve
" them from Popery and arbitrary power, as also concern-
" ing your accessions to the Crown:

" The Governor of this, your Majesties' Colony, by the
" advice of his Council, gave order for the proclaiming
" both your Majesties in each respective town in this your
" colony, which accordingly was done in most solemn man-
" ner, with all alacrity, beseeching the God of Heaven
" to continue your Majesties with a long and prosperous
" reign, not at all doubting but your Majesties will take
" care of all your subjects in this your dominion of New Eng-
" land, as opportunity shall present, that they may be not
" only freed from arbitrary power, but also may enjoy their
" lands and other ancient rights and privileges; and there-
" fore we humbly petition your Most Excellent Majesties'
" grace and favor towards us, your most humble subjects
" and supplicants, that you would please, being *Pater Patrio*
" *Nostro*, to extend your fatherly care in the granting a
" confirmation to our Charter, which, although it was sub-
" mitted to his late Majesty, nevertheless it was not con-
" demned nor taken from us; and therefore, since the late
" revolution, concerning Sir Edmond Andros, his being de-
" posed from the government, we, your Majesties' subjects,
" being destitute of government, saw cause, under grace
" and favor, to reassume the government, according to our

"Charter, the first of May last past, being the Election day appointed by our said Charter, in which Assembly it was ordered: that the former Governor, Deputy Governor, and Assistants that were in place in the year of our Lord, 1686, before the coming over of Sir Edmond Andros, our late Governor, should be established in their respective places for the year ensuing, or further order from England, since which time Sir Edmond Andros made his escape from his confinement in your Majesties' Colony of Massachusetts, into Rhode Island, where he was speedily seized and secured until the Governor and Council of Massachusetts Colony demanded him, by Commissioners sent for that purpose. And accordingly we, the Deputy Governor and some of the Assistants, gave special order for his return, taking care that all moderation should be used in the conveyance of him; and we humbly conceive it hath been a great Providence of God, in this Revolution, to prevent New England from partaking in Ireland's miseries.

"May it please your Excellent Majesties, your transcendant love and favor extended toward us hath so radicated itself in our hearts never to be forgotten, that it obliges us to offer up ourselves, lives and fortunes to be at your Majesties' service, beyond the power of any commands. And we beg the God of Heaven to give both your Majesties a long and prosperous reign over us, and we humbly desire that your Majesties will be pleased to cause us to be enrolled among your loving subjects.

"Dated at Newport, on Rhode Island, your Majesties Colony of Rhode Island and Providence Plantations, in New England, January the 30th, 1689-90. Subscribed by us, your loyal subjects, and most humble supplicants.

"(Signed) "JOHN COGGESHALL, Deputy Governor.
"JOHN EASTON, Assistant.

"EDWARD THURSTON, Assistant.
"JOHN GREENE, "
"GEORGE LAWTON, "
"JOSEPH JENCKES, "
"BENJAMIN SMITH, " "
[R. I. Col. Rec., Vol. 3, pp. 258-9.]

An abstract from a letter from Mr. Francis Brinley, merchant, dated the 22d February, 1689-90, to his son, Mr. Thomas Brinley, merchant, in London:

"At New York, Jacob Leisler rules at his will and
"pleasure, puts in prison whom he pleases, and there keeps
"them. We are here in great confusion. John Cogge-
"shall styles himself Deputy Governor, and John Greene,
"of Warwick, calls himself Assistant (both being of the
"Governor's Council), intend next week to call a General
"Assembly, and to rule by the sword. It is high time his
"Majesty would settle a government over New England.
"We can never govern ourselves with justice nor impar-
"tiality. Unless there be a good government established
"here, as in the other Plantations, I must remove.

"27th do. This day our Deputy Governor and Assist-
"ant, within mentioned, with their Assembly, sat, and be-
"cause Walter Clarke (their Governor) refused to act,
"they chose another Governor, which was Ch'r Almy,
"who, refusing, they chose Henry Bull, who accepts and
"serves.

"Three days since we heard that a town above Albany
"was cut off by the French and Indians, where seventy
"persons were killed, the rest carried captives."
[R. I. Col. Rec., Vol. 3, p. 259, from J. Carter Brown's Manuscripts, Vol. 5, No. 268.]

Again I quote from Prince Society's Andros Tracts, Vol. 3, p. 99, a letter, undoubtedly to Gov. Bradstreet, though not superscribed:

"ESTEEMED:—After due Respects, Wee Reseved yours,

"dated Boston, August the 4th, 1689, and doe signifie in
"answer to yours, that Sir Edmund Andros is here under
"Gard in Newport. And that I have somoned the Gen-
"eral Counsell to Consult that affare, of which answer
"will be sent, is all from yours to serve.
"WALTER CLARKE.
"Newport, this fifth daye
"of August, 1689."

The same day, John Coggeshall writes Gov. Bradstreet as follows:

"Newport, on Rhode Island, Aug. 5, 1689.

"HONORED SIR :

"Our Governor not being free to be active in the af-
"fairs concerning Sir Edmond's confinement, or to wright
"to you, eloaging many Reasons why he cannot be active,
"I, having spoken with Captain Church, and read your
"Letter, and finding you have no certaine knowledge
"whether Sir Edmond Andros be secured, I takeing it to
"be my duty (and as I judge this weighty matter concerns
"us all) doe certainly inform you, that Sir Edmond An-
"dros came into our Towne ye 3d day of August, 1689,
"being Satherday, a little after noon, and after much Ag-
"itation of ye Authority and People, it was Concluded by
"ye majority, that it was most safe for ourselves and ye
"whole Country that he should be secured, which was eme-
"diately don (before sunsett) and conducted to Lif't
"Colonel Peleg Sanford's house, the place concluded on
"for his confinement, where he now is, having a consider-
"able gard of soldiers about ye house, both night and day
"ever since (which is noe little charge), expecting what
"you and your Honored Councill will conclude concern-
"ing hime. I suppose Capt. Church will wright more
"large in particulars. I cannot enlarg, being in great
"hast. My humble service presented.
"Your real friend and servant,
"JOHN COGGESHALL, Dep't. Gov."

These papers give all the light which seems accessible, on the peculiar position of Walter Clarke, at this period. Evidently he had so far become "functus officio" as to leave all the responsibility to the Deputy, also apparently the Assistants, Newberry, Fenner and Arnold, had similar scruples to his, as their signatures are wanting to the address to their Majesties, as well as their presence at the session of the Assembly, February 26th following. In this address reference is made to an Assembly held May 1, 1689 (of which Assembly no record exists, unless as I shall hereafter show) and which continued in office the Governor and other officers, elected in 1686; probably the dissatisfaction on the part of the Governor and some of the Assistants grew out of the absence of the usual forms and the election by the freemen as required under the charter.

Mr. Brinley's letter of Feb. 22, 1689-90, is quite significant. He says: "John Coggeshall styles himself Deputy Governor, and John Greene, of Warwick, calls himself Assistant (both being of the Governor's Council)", meaning clearly Sir Edmond's council. Now there is no evidence that John Greene, though named of the council, ever accepted the position or acted in it, or took the oath under which Coggeshall and some of the others were bound; in fact, Coggeshall had generally been present at the quarter sessions for Rhode Island, as had Fenner.

Mr. Brinley also says: "We are in great confusion," they intend to rule by the sword, and "unless there be a good government established here, as in the other plantations, I must remove." Herein Mr. Brinley expresses the sentiments of his party, which had always had considerable strength on Rhode Island, and still more in King's Province, and which in all emergencies had inclination and power to embarrass and obstruct the growth and prevalence of popular ideas. With this party and these

views, Walter Clarke could by no means have any thing in common. Mr. Brinley being largely interested in Atherton lands, and a near relative of the Coddingtons, was always consistent in his conduct and views, and was very naturally one of the first to welcome the accession to power of Sir Edmond Andros, and was the prominent figure in his administration of Rhode Island affairs. No wonder he was annoyed and disgusted by the explosion of a scheme in which he was a principal actor.

In the matter of the recapture of Sir Edmond in Newport, we may suppose that he was induced to seek that place as his Zoar, from his knowledge of the importance and numbers of his friends and sympathizers in that community, and without doubt he was entertained by Major Peleg Sanford (whose house we may say, in passing, was the corner of Broad and Farewell streets, now standing opposite the State House), as an honored guest and friend, and not as, in any sense, his captor or jailer, he being, evidently, his warm partisan.

Walter Clarke, it seems, had received a letter from Gov. Bradstreet, and replies, without expressing himself in any very positive manner, that he will make his wishes known to the General Council. So far as we can judge, he took no further responsibility in the affair. Sir Edmond was delivered to the Massachusetts authorities chiefly through the Deputy Governor's agency.

The following extract from the records of the General Assembly, May Session, 1686, proves the existence of a duplicate copy of the Charter, at that time, and the disposition of it shows the jealousy with which they sought to guard it:

"Voted, This Assembly having desired the late Deputy
"Governor, now our honored Governor, that, according to
"former order and practice in the colony, the duplicate of

"his majesty's gracious charter be brought to this Assembly, and delivered to our present Deputy Governor, to which our honored Governor consented; and the duplicate sent for, and safely in folio and seal, under the yellow wax, no ways defaced, hath been received, and the same is committed to the care and keeping of our Deputy Governor, Major John Coggeshall, for which our present Governor is discharged thereof." (R. I. Col. Rec., Vol. 3, p. 188.)

There is no record of any act of the Assembly, establishing the order and practice referred to, but the other copy referred to previously as being in charge of the Governor in 1666, "it is committed to the custody of the Governor, William Brenton, for the safe keeping thereof, until the General Assembly shall otherwise order, and subsequently, was reclaimed and recommitted, on every charge." (R. I. Col. Rec., Vol. 2, p. 152.) As in May, 1669, a receipt to Mr. Brenton, for the charter, &c., is recorded (R. I. Col. Rec,. Vol. 2, pp. 243-4), also to Benedict Arnold, May, 1672 (R. I. Col. Rec.,Vol. 2, p. 458), also to Nicholas Easton, in May, 1674 (R. I. Col. Rec., Vol. 2, p. 520), also to Wm. Coddington, in May, 1676 (R. I. C. R., Vol. 2, p. 542), also to Walter Clarke, in 1677 (R. I. C. R., Vol. 2, p. 566), also to Ann Coddington, widow of William, in Nov. 1678 (R.I.C.R.,Vol. 3, p. 25), also to Mary, widow of John Cranston, in March, 1680 (R. I. C. R., Vol. 3, p. 80), also to Peleg Sanford, in May,1683 (R.I. C. R., V. 3, p. 123), also to Wm. Coddington, in May, 1685 (R. I. C. R., V. 3, p. 170), also to Henry Bull, in May, 1686 (R. I. C. R., V. 3, p. 187).

So that the public records show the great care taken of the copy in charge of the Governor, but the duplicate is not so often referred to; it came into possession of the Assembly, through Thomas Ward, one of John Clarke's assigns, Nov. 15, 1678, as appears by receipt on the part

of the colony, from Peleg Sanford, John Coggeshall, John
Sanford, John Albro and Arthur Fenner, and was committed to the keeping of the then present Deputy Governor (R. I. C. R., Vol. 3, p. 25).

The record proceeds as follows:

" February 26, 1689-90. Ordered by the Assembly, that
" Mr. James Greene, Mr. Benedict Arnold, and Mr.
" Edward Thurston, jn'r, are nominated and appointed to
" go to Mr. Walter Clarke, Governor, and to Mr. Walter
" Newberry, Assistant, and desire them to come to the
" court to-morrow, by eight of the clock, which will be
" the 27th inst., at William Mayes' house, or else give in
" their positive answer, whether they will serve in their
" respective places or no." (R. I. Col. Rec., Vol. 3, p. 260.)

" February 27th, 1689-90.

" Mr. Walter Clarke, and Mr. Walter Newberry, having
" made their appearance, read a paper, wherein it evidently
" appears, they disclaim the government, as also, through
" their neglect in disappearing at the last Assembly appoint-
" ed by the Patent, and called by virtue of a warrant,
" subscribed by Walter Clarke, Governor, to be held the
" last Wednesday in October last past, the said court fail-
" ed, the Assistants of the main being prevented by stormy
" weather, from appearing that day.

" Therefore, for the preventing such inconvenience for
" the future, it is enacted by this Assembly, unanimously,
" to proceed to election of a Governor and Assistants, in
" room of those that refuse to serve.

" The Governor elected, was Mr. Ch'r Almy, who being
" required, refused to serve in the place of a Governor,
" giving satisfactory reasons to the Assembly; whereupon
" the Assembly went to election of another, and chose Mr.
" Henry Bull, Governor, and elected Mr. Benedict Arnold,
" Assistant, in the room of Walter Newberry; and Mr.
" John Coggeshall, Assistant, being sent for, appeared and

" refused to serve. Whereupon the court proceeded to
" election of an Assistant in his room, and chose Mr. Ch'r
" Almy, Assistant, and then proceeded to engage the Gov-
" ernor, Deputy Governor, and all the aforesaid Assistants,
" who accordingly received the same ; as also elected a
" General Treasurer, viz. : John Holmes, who was also en-
" gaged.
  "Ordered, that Mr. Joseph Jenckes, Assistant,Mr. Bene-
"dict Arnold, Assistant, Mr. Christopher Almy, Assistant,
"Mr. James Greene, Mr. Jonathan Holmes, and Mr. Joseph
"Clarke, Deputies, the General Recorder, the General
"Sergeant, and his deputy, are, by this Assembly, appoint-
"ed and empowered to go to the late Governor, Walter
"Clarke, Esquire, and demand and receive the Charter,
"and all other papers and things in his custody, belonging
"to this Colony, and in behalf of this Assembly, to give
" a discharge for what they receive, and return the
"premises to this Assembly.
  "The return of the Committee is, that Walter Clarke,
"above said, refuseth to deliver the Charter and Writings,
"but declared that it was in a chest, and he would give
"leave to take it, whereupon the Committee were order-
"ed and empowered to take it accordingly ; but their re-
"turn was, that he refused to let the Charter go, unless
"the Committee would forcibly open the chest and take
"it." [R. I. Col. Rec., Vol. 3, pp. 260, 261.]
  Inasmuch as Major John Coggeshall had been Deputy Governor in 1686, and had acted as such in 1689, and
was re-elected in 1690,and declined, the John Coggeshall,
Assistant, referred to in the foregoing record, must have
been his son, John Coggeshall, of Portsmouth.
  The next record which I propose to present, is dated
May 1, 1690, but for various reasons, I have arrived at the
conclusion that it should be 1689.
  "The Charter being sent for, from our late Governor,

"Walter Clarke, was produced by gentlemen appointed,
"to the open view of the Assembly, and as carefully re-
"turned to his custody again.

"Voted, It is ordered by a unanimous vote of the As-
"sembly, that Mr. Joseph Jenckes, Mr. Benedict Arnold,
"Mr. Isaac Lawton, Mr. James Greene, are appointed a
"Committee to go to Mr. Thomas Ward, and demand and
"receive all the Records belonging to this Colony of
"Rhode Island and Providence Plantations, and upon re-
"ceipt thereof, to give him a discharge for what they re-
"ceive.

"They being returned, do declare that they have de-
"manded the said records, and Mr. Thomas Ward refuseth
"to deliver them without they be taken out his hands by
"distraint.

"Voted, It is ordered by a unanimous vote of the As-
"sembly, *nemine contradicente*, that our former Gover-
"nor, Walter Clarke, our former Deputy Governor, and
"all the former Assistants of this Colony, that were in
"place in the year of Our Lord 1686, at the coming over
"of Sir Edmond Andros, our late Governor, that the said
"Governor, Deputy Governor and Assistants, are con-
"firmed and established in their respective places for the
"year ensuing, or further order from England.

"Voted, That a Recorder and Sergeant be elected, our
"former Recorder (John Sanford) being deceased.

"Mr. Weston Clarke chosen Recorder."

The same day, May 1, 1690, an act was passed, reinstat-
ing all the officers and confirming all acts and orders, civil
and military, as they existed in the year 1686, and on the
same day was issued a declaration resuming the government under the charter, &c. [R. I. Col. Rec., Vol. 3, pp.
267-8-9.]

On the 6th of May, 1690, the Assembly met, Henry

Bull being Governor, and John Coggeshall, Deputy Governor, at the house of William Mayes, Newport. Mr. Bull and Mr. Coggeshall being reëlected on the 7th, both declined, when John Easton was elected Governor and John Greene, Deputy Governor, and both accepted. [R. I. Col. Rec., Vol. 4, pp. 269-70-71.]

Now, it is not conceivable that after the transactions of February preceding, Mr. Clarke should have been again asked to serve, or that such a vote should have been passed six days before an election; besides Henry Bull appears on the record as governor, May 6th, when the Assembly convened; nor would the declaration of resumption apply at that late date, after the government had been administered for a year by Deputy Governor Coggeshall and the board of Assistants. Besides, the name of Weston Clarke appears as Recorder in the record of February proceedings; and John Sanford, the Recorder of 1686, having died in 1687, Clarke must have been appointed in May, no other session having been held in the interval.

The claiming of the records also from Thomas Ward, presumably the executor or administrator of John Sanford, who died in 1687, was the proper work of the session of May 1, 1689, which the petition of the Governor and Council to King William and Queen Mary, of January 30, 1689-90, expressly states, was held, and describes its action as precisely coincident with the record in question. The conclusion is therefore irresistible, that the record of May 1, 1690, is transposed and misdated, and should be credited to 1689.

There seems to have been also in the mind of Thomas Ward, some hesitation about accepting the authenticity of the revivified rump of the old Charter government, and although, in the Providence of God, the influences surrounding the throne were favorable to the colonists, and

their acts were finally justified, it is easy to see that wise men may have hesitated, in the dark, to trust themselves to that contingency, although their own inclinations were not unfavorable to the movement.

Walter Clarke certainly called the session in May, 1689, also the session proposed in October, which fell through; clearly in each case he declined any further responsibility, not from disaffection, but most probably from a sense of the obligation he had come under, to the administration of Sir Edmond Andros.

I submit, therefore, that the conduct of Walter Clarke in this time of sore trial, was not worthy of censure, but, though he showed no heroism, as he laid claim to none, was worthy a man of wisdom and honor, and consistent with the peaceful practices of the society whose tenets he had adopted.

DECLARATION OF THE COLONY OF RHODE ISLAND.

"We, the assembly of freemen of the Colony of Rhode
"Island and Providence Plantations, in New England, be-
"ing assembled this first day of May, 1689, do with all
"due and humble submission make our humble address to
"the present supreme power of England, declaring that
"the late government of the dominion of New England,
"whereof Edmond Andros was Governor-in-Chief, as we
"are certainly informed, is now silenced by reason, his
"person as well as some of his council are seized and con-
"fined within the limits of Boston, in New England, for
"what cause best known to themselves. By which over-
"ture, we, the freemen aforesaid, were void of govern-
"ment, the consequence whereof appearing dangerous, we
"have thought it most safe for the keeping of the peace
"of our colony to lay hold of our charter privileges, es-
"tablishing our officers according to their former station,
"hoping and not questioning but through grace and favor,

"our said charter according to the extent of it, may be
"confirmed unto us, we being a small colony, distinct from
"other colonies, which our predecessors, through much
"difficulty, procured, having been a poor, distressed and
"persecuted people, as can largely be demonstrated, if
"need require. Further, we humbly pray, if any ill af-
"fected person should endeavor to suggest any complaint
"against us, it may be so favorably constructed and sus-
"pended, so that we may make our defense. Thus hum-
"bly prostrating ourselves at your feet, humbly praying
"that forasmuch as we are not only ignorant of what title
"should be given in this overture, but also not so rhetori-
"cal as becomes such personages. Therefore, we humbly
"beg pardon and remain your humble supplicants and
"servants.

"Signed in behalf of the assembly aforesaid,
"WALTER CLARKE,
"JOHN GREENE,
"WALTER NEWBERRY.

"From Newport, on Rhode Island, in the Colony of Rhode Island and Providence Plantations, in New England, the 1st of May, 1689." [R. I. Col. Rec., Vol. 3, p. 226, from John Carter Brown's Manuscripts, No. 14, Vol. 3.]

It would appear from the above address, that Walter Clarke and Walter Newberry were in full sympathy with their associates, in the resumption of their powers under the charter, in the emergency in which the deposition of King James and the vacation and durance of Sir Edmond Andros had placed them; and this gives some color to another theory, perhaps equally tenable, viz.: that the recapture of Sir Edmond at Newport, and his return to the authorities of Massachusetts on their requisition, in August, 1689, was regarded by them as an unjustifiable measure, and as a gross breach of the laws of hospitality, on the part

of a community in whose general character and conduct I take no little pride, towards an unfortunate man, who, so far as appears, had held relations with them of a personally friendly character, and had thrown himself upon their generosity in time of sore tribulation. We cannot but admit that this was a high-handed measure, independently of its sentimental aspect, and it was aggravated by the fact of its being done at the behest of Massachusetts, which, in their declaration of May 1st they had pretty plainly hinted at, when they speak of their distressed and persecuted condition, and whose conduct in relation to Sir Edmond's captivity they had disclaimed in the phase, "for what cause, best known to themselves."

In case of this being the cause of the failure of Walter Clarke and Walter Newberry to continue in their positions, their dissatisfaction was entirely justified by the acquittal and release of Sir Edmond, immediately on his arrival in England, on the ground of there being no evidence of his having done anything contrary to his instructions; fortunately the disposition of the new government was friendly to the colonies, and they incurred no further penalty or reproof, but certainly no greater outrage could have been offered to the laws which guard the private rights of Englishmen, than was visited on Sir Edmond for carrying out the instructions of his sovereign.

The fact that W. Clarke's failure to appear at the proposed session of the Assembly in October, 1689, called by himself, is the first occasion in which he shows a disposition not to fulfil the duties of Governor, fortifies this explanation of his motives.

A short correspondence with Gov. Fletcher, of New York, in May, 1696, shows that Gov. Clarke had luminous views on public affairs, and stood firmly by the interest of Rhode Island; it is in relation to the quota of men claim-

ed from Rhode Island for service in other colonies. [R. I.
Col. Rec., Vol. 3, pp. 315-16-17, from N. Y. Documents,
Vol. 4, pp. 155-6.]

It is creditable to Walter Clarke, that he incurred a
great deal of censure from Edward Randolph and Earl
Bellomont in their contest with the colonial authorities
about the close of the century. A very voluminous correspondence may be found in the 3d Vol. R. I. Col. Rec.,
mostly taken from John Carter Brown's manuscripts, which
want of time forbids me to examine in detail, in which
abundant evidence is afforded of the sturdy adhesion of
Gov. Clarke to the rights and interests of the colony, and
the fearless manner in which he asserted them. I cannot
forbear, however, to inflict on you two or three documents,
so eminently do they serve my present purpose.

PELEG SANFORD TO THE BOARD OF TRADE, &c.

"NEWPORT, Jan. 31, 1697-8.

" May it please your Lordships : I account myself bound
" in duty to give your Lordships an account, that on the
" 7th day of this present month of January, I received
" from the hands of Jahleel Brenton, Esq., his Majesty's
" Commission, dated at his High Court of Admiralty of
" England, the 26th day of June last, to me, to hold and
" execute the office of Judge of the Court of Admiralty
" in this Colony of Rhode Island, &c. Wherefore, in obe-
" dience to his Majesty's pleasure therein (and that I
" might be enabled and qualified to discharge that trust
" reposed in me), on the 12th day of this said month of
" January, I went to the General Assembly of this Colony,
" then assembled at this town of Newport, and there pre-
" sented the said commission to Walter Clarke, Esq., Gov-
" ernor of this Colony, then sitting in that court, desiring
" their publication of said commission and their assistance
" to me in the execution thereof, and that they would ad-

"minister to me the oath for my faithful executing the
"said office. The said Clarke replied, that they would
"consider thereof, and sent the said Commission to the
"lower House, but before the lower House had read the
"same, the said Clarke privately left the upper House
"and went to the lower House, and there acquainted
"them that such a Commission was sent to Peleg San-
"ford, as was a violation and infringement of their charter
"right and privileges, and if they allowed thereof, he
"would take his leave of them, and there would be no
"more choice or election, according to their charter.
"But the said lower House returned that Commission
"to the said Clarke, or upper House, not being prevailed
"with to do anything in opposition thereto.

"Soon after this, the said Clarke adjourned the said
"Assembly, but detains from me the said Commis-
"sion, and positively refuses to deliver the same, though
"I have several times demanded it of him. I am humbly
"of opinion, that if ever he should restore to me the said
"Commission, those persons at present in government
"here will refuse to administer to me an oath for exe-
"cuting the said office, &c., without which I dare not pre-
"sume to act therein.

"I humbly submit this whole matter unto your Lord-
"ships' great wisdom, and remain your Lordships' most
"humble servant. (Signed)

"PELEG SANFORD."

REPORT OF PELEG SANFORD, FRANCIS BRINLEY, AND
JAHLEEL BRENTON, TO THE KING.

"May it please your Majesty: Whereas your Majesty
"by your Commission, under the great seal of England,
"bearing date at Westminster, the 23d day of May, in the
"eighth year of your Majesty's reign, was graciously pleased
"to authorize and appoint Edward Randolph, Peleg San-

"ford, Francis Brinley, Jahleel Brenton, Nathaniel By-
"field, Thomas Newton, Esq., or any five of the members
"of the Council, and the Collector of the King's customs,
"for the time being, within your Majesty's Colony of
"Rhode Island, or any three or more of them, to admin-
"ister to the Governor or Commander-in-Chief of your
"Majesty's said Colony (by virtue of several acts of Par-
"liament mentioned in the said Commission), a solemn
"oath to do their utmost, that all the clauses, matters and
"things contained in several acts of Parliament (mention-
"ed also in said Commission), shall be punctually and
"*bona fide* observed, so far as appertains to the said Gover-
"nor or Commander-in-Chief respectively, as in the said
"Commission, and the several acts of Parliament therein
"mentioned, is at large expressed.

"In obedience to your Majesty's commands, we, your
"Majesty's said Commissioners, whose names are hereunto
"subscribed, do humbly report to your Majesty, that on
"the 17th day of this present month of January, at the
"town of Newport, in the aforesaid Colony of Rhode
"Island, we went to the dwelling house of Walter Clarke,
"Governor of said Colony, and did then and there show
"to the said Walter Clarke your Majesty's said Commis-
"sion, and the oath which is mentioned in, and wrote
"down after the said Commission, and did also offer and
"tender to the said Walter Clarke, the said oath, which
"oath the said Walter Clarke did positively refuse to take.
"Likewise, on the 21st day of this same month of January,
"we went to the said dwelling house of the said Walter
"Clarke, and did then also show to him your Majesty's
"said Commission, and did demand of him if he would
"take the said oath, and the said Walter Clarke did then
"also, positively refuse to take the said oath. Of which,

" in all humble obedience to your Majesty's said Commis-
" sion and commands to us, we make this report.
" Your Majesty's most loyal and most dutiful subjects,
  (Signed) "PELEG SANFORD,
        " FRANCIS BRINLEY,
        " JAHLEEL BRENTON.
"Dated at Newport, this 31st day of January, 1697-8."

JAHLEEL BRENTON TO THE BOARD OF TRADE, ON RHODE ISLAND AFFAIRS:

BOSTON, March the 8th, 1697-8.

"May it please your Lordships: On the 8th of Decem-
" ber I arrived in this Bay, and some little time after my
" arrival, I went to Rhode Island, and there delivered to
" the Governor and company, those letters, your Lordships
" were pleased to entrust me with the conveyance of. I
" also brought with me a Commission, under the great
" seal, to administer to the Governor of Rhode Island an
" oath, according to several acts of Parliament, made for
" the Plantation trade, which the said Governor (who is a
" Quaker) hath refused to take. Enclosed, I humbly
" transmit to your Lordships the report concerning the
" same.

" I likewise brought with me a Commission to Peleg
" Sanford, Esq., to hold and execute the office of Judge of
" Admiralty in the said Colony, and a Commission to Na-
" thaniel Coddington, Esq., to execute the office of Regis-
" ter of the said Court, both which commissions having
" been showed to the said Clarke, requiring his assistance
" in the execution thereof, &c., the said Clarke detained
" and kept the same; the said Sanford, by his letter en-
" closed, hath humbly acquainted your Lordships there-
" with.

" And I think it my duty, likewise, to acquaint your
" Lordships, that the said Clarke, in the month of May,

"1696, was chosen Governor of that Colony, and in June following he refused to subscribe the association, which is required by the act made for the better security of his Majesty's Royal person and government, though the same was generally subscribed by others in that colony, at that time.

"I am humbly of opinion, that if his Majesty would be pleased to grant forth a Commission to such persons in that Colony (as to his Majesty, in his wisdom, shall seem meet), empowering them to examine upon oath and make report of these matters to his Majesty in Council, and that if the said Clarke were commanded to make his appearance, and there answer for the same, it would deter others from the like practice for the future; but if he should be no ways called to account for these facts, his Majesty's loyal subjects in that Colony will be utterly discouraged.

"And I further beg leave to acquaint your Lordships that I am humbly of opinion, it would much conduce to his Majesty's service, and the good of his subjects in the Colony of Rhode Island, that the government of that Colony were commanded to print all such laws, as have been there made, and are now in force. For they are so meanly kept, and in blotted and defaced books (having never yet, any of them been printed), that few of his Majesty's subjects there, are at present able to know what they are.

"All which is most humbly submitted to your Lordships' great wisdom, by your Lordships' most obedient servant.   (Signed)

"JAHLEEL BRENTON."

[R. I. Col. Rec., Vol. 3, pp. 229-30-31, from John Carter Brown's manuscripts, Vol. 3, Nos. 24-27.]

I have quoted these documents at length, because they are not only particularly useful as throwing a strong light

upon the character and political status of Walter Clarke, but also exhibit the animus of those who aided the minions of royalty, in the prosecution of their persistent warfare upon the advancing tide of liberal and humanitarian progress.

I submit that these documents give no support to that estimate of Walter Clarke, implied by the expression, "wavering"; on the contrary, hardihood would better express the attributes which he exhibited at this period. It is true, that Mr. Brenton says "he was a Quaker," implying thereby, that his objection to taking an oath was the actuating principle of his conduct, but this could not explain his withholding Mr. Sanford's commission, or his efforts to induce the house of deputies to repudiate it, using the argument that it was a blow aimed at their charter rights and privileges.

I claim, that whether of his own volition, or prompted by the indomitable spirit of John Greene, then deputy governor, who according to the constantly reiterated representations of the royal agents, was the arch rebel of them all, Walter Clarke stands forth as the boldest champion of human rights, of his time; that seeing in the obligation required of him, to support the acts of Parliament in relation to trade and navigation, an encroachment upon the rights and interests of the colonies, he exhibited the sublimest heroism in resisting them, and initiated the opposition which continued to disturb the eighty years of colonial existence yet remaining, and only culminated into fruition, in the reign of George the Third, under the stimulus of more direct attacks.

If I am thought to use unreasonably strong expressions, let it be remembered, that not only was Rhode Island infinitesimally limited in territorial area, but also in population; that the rival claims of Connecticut and Rhode Island

to jurisdiction over King's Province, were not yet definitively settled, and the tract of three miles in width on the east side of the bay, comprising the present towns of Little Compton, Tiverton, Bristol, Warren, Barrington, and Cumberland, were not assigned to Rhode Island, until 1747, fifty years later; that in New England, only Connecticut and Rhode Island retained the privilege of electing their own governor, Massachusetts having succumbed and never having enjoyed that right, from the vacation of Andros to the breaking out of the revolution, and being at this time under the domination of that arch enemy of colonial rights, Earl Bellomont, who with aid of his able and astute and unscrupulous coadjutor, Edward Randolph, abetted by the factious element in their midst, was moving heaven and earth to find or create causes of complaint against the colonists, and pressing them upon the attention of the royal council and the board of trade, with all the bitterness of personal feeling, and all the strength of class prejudice, and all the influences of courtly association.

Remembering all this, I unhesitatingly affirm that the fortitude with which Walter Clarke, representing as he did, the humblest (in the eyes of the world) community on the face of the earth, defied the royal authority in the interest, as he believed, of truth and justice, is one of the grandest exhibitions of manly courage in the history of our race.

Walter[2] Clarke was born 1640, and died May 22, 1714, aged 74 years. He married,
1. Content Greenman ; she died March 27, 1665-6, aged 30 years.
2. Hannah Scott ; she died July 24, 1681, aged 39 years.
3. Freeborn Hart, widow; she died Jan. 10, 1709-10, ag. 72 y.
4. Sarah Gould, widow, Aug. 31, 1711.

By first wife, Content he had :
1. Content (probably), who married Philip Harwood.

2. A son not named ; died young.
3. Mary[3], born Jan. 11, 1661, married, first, Daniel Gould ; second, Ralph Chapman, Jr.

By second wife, Hannah, he had :

4. Hannah[3], born Oct. 28, 1667; died Oct. 22, 1722; married Thomas Rodman, third wife, Nov. 26, 1691.
5. Catharine[3], born Sept. 6, 1671, died January 25, 1752, aged 83 years; married, first, James Gould; second, Nathaniel Sheffield.
6. Frances[3], born January 17, 1673, may be second wife of James Hart.
7. Jeremiah[3], born Feb. 21, 1675, died young.
8. Deliverance[3], born July 4, 1678, died Oct. 8, 1732; married George Cornell, Portsmouth, Jan, 18, 1699.

Freeborn, the third wife of Walter Clarke, was widow of Thomas Hart, and daughter of Roger Williams. She had two sons, Thomas and James Hart, and one daughter Mary Hart, who was the wife of Gov. Samuel Cranston, who was Walter Clarke's nephew and Jeremiah Clarke's grandson.

Walter Clarke's sons both died unmarried; he, therefore, had no descendants to perpetuate his name, but by the female branches his progeny is very numerous. All the Rodmans and their collaterals are his descendants in Rhode Island and its neighborhood, particularly in Providence Newport, and New Bedford, except those in Narragansett, who may be from Thomas Rodman, 2d, who was a son of Thomas Rodman by a former wife, and who settled in Narragansett.

By his daughter Catharine, who married James Gould, he was the ancestor of many prominent people in Newport and Providence, among whom are Ellerys, Brinleys, Johnstons, and Almys.

By Deliverance, who married George Cornell, his descendants are very numerous, among whom may be enu-

merated the late Major Henry Bull, of Newport, for many years conspicuous in Rhode Island affairs, and noted for his thorough knowledge of Rhode Island colonial history, before such matters had attracted much attention, as well as Stanhopes, Engses, Littlefields and many others. The second son of Jeremiah Clarke 1st, named also Jeremiah[2], freeman 1666, was deputy from Newport from 1696 to 1705 inclusive, and otherwise is not prominent in the public records. His progeny is exceedingly numerous, and includes among others the family of the late Audley Clarke, Esq.,with Gardners, Fowlers, &c.,of Newport; and of Providence, several of the oldest and best known families are from Jeremiah Clarke[2]; by his grand-daughter Frances Sanford, who married Deputy Governor John Gardner :

1. Deputy Governor Gardner's daughter Frances married William Benson, and was the mother of George Benson, who was of the firm of Brown, Rogers & Benson, now Brown & Ives, if I am corretly informed. Mr. Benson is fresh in the memory of some of you, and has descendants among you.
2. Another daughter of Deputy Governor Gardner, Lydia, married William Rodman. Her son, Captain William Rodman, was for many years a prominent man in Providence,and his family well known. Her daughter Elizabeth married John Rogers, another of the original members of the firm of Brown & Ives, and through her, the honored president of this society, Lieutenant-Governor Arnold, Hon. Horatio Rogers, Rev. John Rogers, and probably many others, better known to you than to me, are enrolled among the family of Jeremiah Clarke. Her daughter Elizabeth married Stephen Hopkins, whose descendants, if there be any, shall be welcome to the family. Singularly enough, the Rodmans above mentioned, derive from Jeremiah

Clarke, through both sons, Walter[2] and Jeremiah[2].
3. Another daughter of Deputy Governor Gardner, Elizabeth, married Captain Peter Wanton; he, also, was a well known citizen of Providence. Of her daughters, Frances married Samuel Snow; Mary married ——— Hopkins. Of their descendants I know nothing.

Latham[2], third son of Jeremiah[1], married Hannah Wilbour, of Samuel, probably about 1772 or 3, and by her had four daughters and three sons, as follows, viz:

1. Abigail[3], married Samuel Thurston.
2. Elizabeth[3], married John Stanton.
3. Mary[3], married Joseph Fry.
4. Ann[3], married William Wood.
5. Samuel[3], married Mary Coggeshall, of Daniel, Portsmouth; his son Joseph, was General Treasurer from May, 1761, to May, 1792, 31 years.
6. William, married ——— Knight,
7. Latham, married Hope ———.

Latham[2] Clarke married, second, Ann Newberry, the widow of Walter Newberry, Sept. 20, 1698; he died June 1, 1719, aged 74 years; she died Feb. 19, 1732, aged 80 years, 6 months. Between 1681 and 1690, he was for several years deputy from Portsmouth, otherwise he does not appear in public affairs, but is said to have been a famous minister among the Friends. The Goulds of Newport are from Latham[2], by Mary[4], of Samuel[3], who married Stephen Wanton[3], of Michael[2], of Edward[1]. John Stanton Gould, late of New York State, derives a second strain from Jeremy Clarke, through Hannah Rodman, daughter of Walter Clarke.

Weston,[2] the fourth son of Jeremiah Clarke, was born July 2, 1648, died after 1714. He was freeman, Newport, Oct., 1670; Keeper of Weights and Measures, May 5, 1675;

Moderator of Electoral Assembly, May 2, 1676; Attorney General, May 5, 1680, 1684, 1685; he was Recorder, equivalent to Secretary of State, in 1690-1, and from May, 1695, to May, 1714: in all, 20 years. His name appears several times in matters of routine, but never as if he were a leading character in public affairs. He married Dec. 25, 1668, Mary Easton, of Peter and Anne (Coggshall) Easton, and had:

1. Mary,[3] married James Hart; born Jan. 11, 1669.
2. John,[3] born Sept. 15, 1672; died soon.
3. Weston,[3] born Feb. 18, 1674; died soon.
4. Weston,[3] born April 15, 1677; died young.
5. Jeremiah,[3] born Nov. 29, 1685; died Jan. 3, 1689, aged 3 years, 3 months, 24 days.
6. Ann,[3] born ———— ————, married Thomas Hicks, Portsmouth.
7. Patience.
   His wife died Nov. 16, 1690, aged 42 years, and he married, second, Rebecca Easton, widow of Peter, Jr., and daughter of Edward Thurston, Nov. 21, 1691. She died Sept. 16, 1737, aged 75 years, 4 months. They had
8. Jeremiah[3], born July 27, 1692; died Sept. 3, 1756.
9. Mary,[3] born Feb. 8, 1693-4.
10. Elizabeth,[3] born Nov. 5, 1695.
11. Weston,[3] born Aug. 25, 1697; died June 22, 1737.

James[2] Clarke, the fifth and last son of Jeremiah[1] Clarke, was born in 1649, and died Dec. 1, 1736, aged 87 years. His wife was Hope Power, daughter of Nicholas, of Providence. She died Feb. 27, 1717, aged 67 years. He was a Baptist minister, and pastor of the Second Baptist Church, for 35 years. He does not appear to have been prominent in secular affairs.

James and Hope Clarke had
1. Hope,[3] born December 29, 1673.

Jeremy Clarke's Family.

2. Jonathan,[3] born 1681; died May 22, 1758, aged 72 years.

Jonathan,[3] married first, Amy ———; she died Feb. 16, 1735, aged 48 years; married second, Ann ———; she died Jan. 20, 1764, aged 60 years.

Jonathan[3] had three children, who died young, and not improbably many others, as equally probably had his father. This is all I have been able to pick up relative to James[2] and Hope Clarke's family, although I have long had especial interest in it, and given it much attention.

From the daughters of Jeremiah[1] Clarke are all the descendants of Randall Holden, and John Cranston, and very many of Caleb Carr, and their female branches.

To conclude, I trust I have worthily performed a filial duty, being myself a descendant from Randall Holden, as, by a somewhat singular coincidence, my wife is from John Cranston.

www.ingramcontent.com/pod-product-compliance
Lightning Source LLC
Chambersburg PA
CBHW031119160426
43192CB00008B/1043